# WHAT LIFE'S ALL ABOUT

*What Life's All About* © 2017 by Laurie Ciulla & Debi Plasker

ISBN: 978-1-944037-65-9

Book design by Colin Rolfe, Laurie Ciulla & Debi Plasker
Art by Debi Plasker  www.artzeedesigns.net

Epigraph Books
22 East Market St., Suite 304
Rhinebeck, NY 12572
(845) 876-4861
www.epigraphps.com

# WHAT LIFE'S ALL ABOUT

Words by LAURIE CIULLA

Art by DEBI PLASKER

Epigraph Books
Rhinebeck, New York

So you've opened a book,
and put down your device.
What you're touching is PAPER.
What you hear is *advice*.

I know life is **noisy**,

and it's so hard to hear,

but I need you to listen,

SO I'LL TRY TO BE CLEAR.

I just want you to know
that from inside to out –
it's not what you think,
this 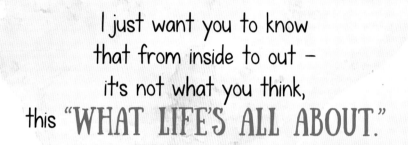"WHAT LIFE'S ALL ABOUT."

Some people might say,
"work hard – do your best,
and keep yourself busy.
There's no time for rest."

But it's not about **busy**.
It's not about things.
It's not about MONEY,
or what money brings.

It's not what you have,
or the way that you look,
or the **grades** that you get,
or the **tests** that you took.

It's none of these things
that matter at all.
I couldn't care less
if you're **round** or you're TALL.

What matters the most
is not **what you do** –
**who you are** is what matters.
It's what makes you YOU!

Are you kind and forgiving,
and honest and strong?
If you hurt someone's feelings,
can you admit that you're wrong?

Do you care? Do you cry?
Do you know how you feel?
Do you FALL, make mistakes,
and trust you can heal?

Do you know that mistakes
are part of the deal,
and that no one is **perfect**,
and perfect's not real?

You should also remember that we're on the same page. It's not **all** about you. Life's not a stage.

You're not a performer, or the **star** of the show, though there are plenty of folks who might tell you so.

We all sort of wish
we could say what we please,
and be who we are
with **joy** and with *ease*.

But it's not always easy.
We're not all the same.
What a thrill it would be, though,
to just **BE** and not **BLAME**.

You should **love** who you **love**,
and respect all the rest.
Just 'cause it's YOURS
doesn't mean it's THE BEST.

(May I make a suggestion,
if it isn't too late?
Put all bets on **LOVE**.
It runs faster than Hate.)

If you pay close attention,
you'll see what I mean.
We all serve a purpose,
but we're on the SAME TEAM.

I'm no better than you are.
You're no better than **me**,
or the puppy, the old man,
the kid, or the tree.

We're here in this **world**,
sharing this space.
We're all here TOGETHER.
We're all in **one** place!

Let's take care of each other
(this news isn't new).
Keep your heart open
(it's the least we can do).

Remember to wonder,
to hope and be kind.
Life's **twisty** and **turny** –
who knows what you'll find?

These things may seem simple, but they never get old. Be good on the inside, and the rest will **unfold!**

# WHAT LIFE'S ALL ABOUT

So you've opened a book,
and put down your device.
What you're touching is *paper*.
What you hear is *advice*.

I know life is noisy,
and it's so hard to hear,
but I need you to listen,
so I'll try to be clear.

I just want you to know
that from inside to out –
it's not what you think,
this **"what life's all about."**

Some people might say,
"work hard – do your best,
and keep yourself busy.
There's no time for rest."

But it's not about busy.
It's not about things.
It's not about money,
or what money brings.

It's not what you have,
or the way that you look,
or the grades that you get,
or the tests that you took.

It's none of these things
that matter at all.
I couldn't care less
if you're round or you're tall.

What matters the most
is not *what you do* –
*who you are* is what matters.
It's what makes you **YOU!**

Are you kind and forgiving,
and honest and strong?
If you hurt someone's feelings,
can you admit that you're wrong?

Do you care? Do you cry?
Do you know how you feel?
Do you fall, make mistakes,
and trust you can heal?

Do you know that mistakes
are part of the deal,
and that no one is perfect,
and perfect's not real?

You should also remember
that we're on the same page.
It's not *all* about you.
Life's not a stage.

You're not a performer,
or the star of the show,
though there are plenty of folks
who might tell you so.

We all sort of wish
we could say what we please,
and be who we are
with joy and with ease.

But it's not always easy.
We're not all the same.
What a thrill it would be, though,
to just *be* and not *blame*.

You should love who you love,
and respect all the rest.
Just 'cause it's yours
doesn't mean it's the best.

(May I make a suggestion,
if it isn't too late?
Put all bets on Love.
It runs faster than Hate.)

If you pay close attention,
you'll see what I mean.
We all serve a purpose,
but we're on the same team.

I'm no better than you are.
You're no better than me,
or the puppy, the old man,
the kid, or the tree.

We're here in this world,
sharing this space.
We're all here together.
We're all in *one* place!

Let's take care of each other
(this news isn't new).
Keep your heart open
(it's the least we can do).

Remember to wonder,
to hope and be kind.
Life's twisty and turny –
who knows what you'll find?

These things may seem simple,
but they never get old.
Be good on the inside,
and the rest will unfold!

Debi and Laurie both live in New Jersey with their husbands, who, coincidentally, just happen to be brothers. In addition to their shared taste in men, they both share an unhealthy attachment to their children, a penchant for pretty things, and a sincere appreciation for each other's work.

They'd like to thank their families and friends for their relentless support, love, and patience. Both Debi and Laurie are aware that they require an alarming amount of positive feedback and encouragement. Their people never disappoint.

xo